The World of Martial Arts

Sport Karate

By Jim Ollhoff

Visit us at
www.abdopublishing.com

Published by ABDO Publishing Company, 8000 West 78th Street, Suite 310, Edina, MN 55439.
Copyright ©2008 by Abdo Consulting Group, Inc. International copyrights reserved in all countries.
No part of this book may be reproduced in any form without written permission from the publisher.
ABDO & Daughters™ is a trademark and logo of ABDO Publishing Company.

Printed in the United States.

Editor: John Hamilton
Graphic Design: John Hamilton
Cover Design: Neil Klinepier
Cover Photo: John Hamilton
Interior Photos and Illustrations: p 1 rows of trophies, John Hamilton; p 5 two women fighters at Diamond Nationals, John Hamilton; p 6 woman with protective helmet, John Hamilton; p 7 sparring ring, John Hamilton; p 8 scorekeeper, John Hamilton; p 9 children sparring, iStockphoto; p 10 fighters clash, John Hamilton; p 11 judges score points, John Hamilton; p 12 fighters in protective gear, John Hamilton; p 13 fighter blocks an attack, John Hamilton; p 14 (left) fighter kicks, John Hamilton; p 14 (right) fighter punches to head, John Hamilton; p 15 overhead ridge-hand attack scores, John Hamilton; p 16 boy receives trophy, John Hamilton; p 17 point scores to the head, John Hamilton; p 18 Japanese martial artist performs kata, Getty Images; p 20 man performs sword form, John Hamilton; p 21 man performs freestyle form, John Hamilton; p 22 panel of judges reveal scores, John Hamilton; p 23 young woman blue-belt form competitor, Getty Images; p 25 fighters compete in the UFC octagon, Getty Images; p 27 mixed martial arts fighters compete, Getty Images; p 29 fighter wins match with arm bar, Getty Images.

Library of Congress Cataloging-in-Publication Data

Ollhoff, Jim, 1959-
    Sport karate / Jim Ollhoff.
        p. cm. -- (The world of martial arts)
    Includes index.
    ISBN 978-1-59928-984-7
    1. Karate--Juvenile literature. I. Title.

GV1114.3.O57 2008
796.815'3--dc22
                                2007030554

CONTENTS

武 道

COMPETITIONS

Competition has always been a part of martial arts history. In ancient times, when people fought face-to-face on the battlefield, war was the ultimate competition. In those days, when one army battled another, the stakes were very high: losers were killed or enslaved, and winners went home with the spoils of war.

Today, competition takes the form of contests in exciting sport karate tournaments. Usually, a group of schools in a state or region organizes competitions. Each school then brings its students together for the matches. Sometimes a large school or a central organization with many schools will have a competition limited to its own students. This is called an *intramural* tournament. Other times the competition is a national tournament, where martial arts students from all over the world come together to compete.

Do competitions tell us who is the best martial artist? Not always. Many factors affect competitors' performances. They may do poorly because they don't feel good that day. Perhaps they over-trained and are too tired or sore to perform well. Or maybe they are too nervous and stressed to do well at competition level. While tournaments do not always show us the true answer of who is the best, they continue to be very popular. Tournaments are fun, and they give competitors a chance to practice and compare their skills against other martial artists.

This book describes three kinds of sport competition. *Tournament point fighting* is where two martial artists fight with little or no contact. In *form competition*, martial artists compete by showing off their form—a series of prearranged movements. Finally, *mixed martial arts competitions* are a popular form of full-contact fighting. It is similar to boxing, yet uses all the tools of the martial artist.

Above: Two women compete at the 2007 Diamond Nationals World Karate Championships.

TOURNAMENT POINT FIGHTING

Point fighting, also called sparring, is a very popular part of sport karate. Almost all martial arts tournaments have a point-fighting competition. These are usually elimination matches, where a group of contestants pair off. Winners move on to fight the other winners in their division until only one victor remains.

Point fighting mimics actual fighting, but competitors rarely get seriously hurt. Point fighters wear special padding to minimize injuries. The level of contact, how hard competitors may strike each other for points, is determined by the fighters' age and skill level. Most beginners are limited to light contact, with no strikes to the head allowed.

Right: Special foam padding, such as this well-worn helmet, protects point fighters from serious injury.

Advanced competitors, especially black belts, are allowed to punch and kick using medium contact, even to the head.

Tournament leaders often divide children competitors by age as well as belt rank. One of the challenges that tournaments have is adult belt ranking. Each school can create its own rankings by belt color. A green belt might represent a beginner in one school, but represent an advanced belt in another school. It is possible for an advanced student to fight in a beginner match, but this dishonorable trick rarely occurs. Many tournaments solve the issue by having designations like "beginner, intermediate, advanced, and black belts." Usually, students are placed in categories by their individual schools.

Above: Most tournament fights include a center referee and four corner judges who score the match.

Rules

The sparring ring is a square or circle about 15 feet (4.6 m) across. It is often marked by masking tape on the floor. There is one center judge, or referee, who is usually a black belt, or an experienced fighter. The center judge keeps close watch, following the action and stopping the match when a fighter scores a point. The match is also stopped if competitors move out of the ring, or if someone behaves in an unsportsmanlike way.

Point fighting can be so fast and furious that the center judge often can't see every point that scores. To assist, there are usually two or four side judges who stand in the ring corners and help the center judge score points.

At the beginning of a match, two participants line up facing each other. A small strip of red cloth is tied to the back of one fighter's belt. This person is declared the red side, while the other fighter is the white side. The center judge gives a signal, and the fight begins.

Right: A ring scorekeeper keeps track of the winners of each match.

Each match has a timekeeper and a person who keeps score. Matches usually last two minutes. During the fight, if a point is scored the center judge will shout, "Stop!" Competitors quickly go back to their starting point. The center judge then shouts out, "Judges, score!" The side judges hold up a colored flag, red or white, depending on which side they think scored a point. (Sometimes judges simply point at the fighter.) If a majority of judges agree, the fighter is awarded a point by the center judge.

Above: Sparring at tournaments is very popular even among children as young as five years old.

Below: Two fighters clash. Which punch scored first?

Instead of indicating a point, a judge may instead cross arms in the shape of an "X," which means no one scored in that judge's opinion. The side judges also may hold their hand over their eyes, which means their view was blocked.

Only points that are actually seen by a judge count.

Areas that score points are the front of the body, below the neck and above the belt. The side of the body is usually a scoring area, and sometimes the area of the kidneys (in the lower back, above the hips). In some tournaments, the advanced belts may hit the head lightly.

An important job of the center judge is to keep the fighters under control.

Competitors must not strike too hard, or else they will be penalized for "excessive contact." The fighters must have good control of their punches and kicks at all times. If a judge decides a fighter is hitting too hard, especially to the head, then a warning will be issued, or a penalty point will be awarded to the other competitor. Repeated excessive contact results in disqualification.

The center judge may also disqualify someone who is behaving badly. If a competitor is too aggressive or hard-hitting, or uses bad language or shows other kinds of unsportsmanlike conduct, the center judge can disqualify or ban the fighter from the tournament. Sometimes martial artists, most often beginners, will lose their temper in the heat of battle. The center referee's job is to talk to the students and help them refocus.

Above: The center referee and two corner judges (one is not seen in the photo) award a point to the fighter on the left. One judge signals a point for the other fighter, but is overruled. The judge at far left signals that she did not see a punch land.

Participants usually wear their school uniform and belt when they fight. They wear foam protectors over their hands and feet. This protects them as well as their opponents. They also wear shin guards to protect the sensitive bones in the legs. They usually wear elbow pads and rib cage protectors. Male fighters wear groin protectors, and females wear chest protectors. Helmets are required, and many have plastic visors or metal cages to protect the eyes. Mouthguards are always required to protect the teeth of the fighters.

Below: Fighters in full protective gear compete.

STRATEGY

Point fighters learn to move quickly in the ring. They move in, out, and side-to-side. They are always on the move because a moving target is harder to hit. Good fighters keep their hands up to block any incoming punches or kicks. Usually, fighters stand with one leg forward and one leg back so that they are not directly facing their opponents. One hand is usually extended slightly to protect the head, while the other hand protects the body.

Good point fighters always look for an opponent's weakness. If an opponent's hands are held too high, the stomach is open for a punch or kick. If the hands are held too low, the head becomes an inviting target.

Above: Good point fighters know how to block an opponent's attack.

There are three important strategies that good point fighters use: combinations, fakes, and counters. A combination involves two or more techniques performed in rapid succession. Beginning point fighters will often simply move in, throw a punch, and then move back out. Then they will move close again, throw a kick, and then move back out again. This type of simple strategy is easy to defend against because a person can usually block a single punch or kick. However, it is much more difficult to block combinations—two or more techniques thrown one right after the other. An advanced fighter might move in close to the opponent, throw a jab to the head, and then follow immediately with a punch to the stomach. Or, the fighter may throw a low kick followed by a high punch. Good combinations often go high and then low, or from one side of the opponent's body to the opposite side. This technique makes an attack much more difficult for an opponent to defend against.

Below: In the photo at left, the fighter in red kicks to his opponent's midsection, forcing him to drop his hands. In the photo at right, the red fighter immediately follows up with a punch to the head, which scores a point.

Another important strategy is the fake. This means trying to fool an opponent by starting to do one thing, then doing something else instead. For example, a fighter throws a kick at his opponent's midsection, but the opponent brings his arms down and blocks the kick. The fighter throws another hard kick at his opponent's midsection, but it's blocked again. Then the fighter pretends to throw another hard kick, but only extends his leg partway. The opponent might drop his arms again. That's when the fighter changes his attack and throws a kick high toward the opponent's upper body or head, which are now unprotected. The fake, if thrown convincingly, is a very effective way to score.

Above: At the Diamond Nationals tournament, the fighter in red scores with an overhead ridge-hand strike, which is a very effective technique if preceded first by a convincing fake.

Above: A young martial artist receives a trophy for his performance at a karate tournament.

The other important strategy is the counter. This is the most difficult of the three strategies. A counter takes advantage of whatever technique an opponent has thrown. For example, an opponent throws a kick at a fighter, but she quickly steps back so the kick misses. When the opponent pulls her leg back, she is still standing on her other leg and is slightly off balance. The fighter notices this and rushes in with a punch or a combination. Because the opponent is still concentrating on regaining her balance, it's possible that she won't be able to block the counterattack. To succeed, the counter requires good reflexes, a careful eye, and a lot of speed.

TRAINING

Good point fighting takes a lot of practice. Competitors train to move their feet quickly so they can move forward, backward, or to the side in a split second. They practice quick punches and quick kicks. They practice combinations, fakes, and counters. They also practice control—throwing techniques quickly, but stopping before they do serious damage to their sparring partners. No one wants to fight people who have poor control of their punches and kicks. Controlling the amount of force is an important quality for point fighters.

Below: Skilled point fighters use control to score without harming their opponents.

FORM COMPETITION

A form, also sometimes called a *kata*, is a series of prearranged movements done with speed, power, and crispness. A beginner's form might feature only 10 simple techniques—a punch, a kick, turn, a punch, a kick, and so on. An advanced form can include hundreds of movements, with jumping kicks, spins, and rolls. The martial artist executes each movement quickly and strongly, with a split-second stop in-between each movement. A good form has no extra body motion between the movements. The martial artist, for that split second, is absolutely frozen. Then, the next move explodes hard, with power and precision, followed by another quick stop.

Most martial arts tournaments have a form competition. Competitors are judged on their power, speed, and their ability to stop their motion between movements.

Tournaments divide competitors by belt rank and age. Men and women usually compete separately. Form competition is also divided into traditional forms, weapon forms, musical forms, and sometimes a category called creative, or freestyle, forms.

Facing page: A Japanese martial artist performs a kata at a 2006 tournament in Doha, Qatar.

Above: A man performs a traditional Japanese weapon form using two swords: a *katana* (also called a samurai sword) and a shorter *wakizashi*.

Weapon forms are competitions in which martial artists use weapons as part of their form. The most common weapons used in competition are the staff, the nunchaku, and sometimes a kama or tonfa.

Musical forms are performed so that the competitors' movements and techniques are timed with music. The music often makes the movements more dramatic or exciting.

Creative form competition is for those who are doing unique movements in their forms. Usually, these are acrobatic or gymnastic kinds of movements that are incorporated into a traditional type of martial arts routine. Oftentimes, these freestyle forms involve people doing backflips that end with a kick, or gymnastic-like leaps with punches in midair.

Bo staff

Nunchaku

Kama

Tonfa

Left: A martial artist performs a freestyle form in front of the judges at a tournament in Minnesota.

In most tournaments, three to five judges, usually black belts, score the form competitors. The judges weigh the difficulty of the movements, the rank of the competitors, and most importantly, the power and crispness of the movements. Usually the judges give scores between 7 and 10 points, down to a hundredth of a point. For example, one competitor might score 7.45, and the next person, who does a little better, might score 7.75.

Competitors get good at form through practice—weeks, months, and years of practice. Each movement must explode with strength and power, but then stop crisply and completely. When doing a form, the martial artist uses every ounce of energy available. By the end of a good form, the competitor should be exhausted. Martial artists who study form must be very focused. They can't be people who get bored repeating the same movements over and over. They need to push themselves to do the form better and stronger each time.

Below: A panel of judges reveal their scores to a form competitor.

Above: Form competition is very popular at tournaments, even with inexperienced martial artists who have not yet achieved black belts.

MIXED MARTIAL ARTS

In the early 1990s, a few martial artists and promoters began to wonder if people would watch a match that pitted martial artists of different styles against each other. The fighters would use full contact, like boxing. However, instead of just punching, all the techniques of martial arts would be available. Fighters could use punches, kicks, joint-locks, chokes, and so on. This style of fighting became known as mixed martial arts, or MMA.

One of the first mixed martial arts tournaments, called the *Ultimate Fighting Championship*, was held November 12, 1993. Eight men fought in four quarter-finals, and then two semi-finals. Royce Gracie, a Brazilian jiu-jitsu fighter, won the championship.

One of the questions that the fight promoters asked was, "Can a martial artist beat a boxer?" The answer, of course, depends on whose rules the fighters play by. If they use boxing rules, then the boxer will have the advantage. If they play the match with martial arts rules, the martial artist will have the advantage. Still, the promoters were successful at giving the impression that one style of martial arts was going to be pitted against another style. Most of the early fighters only knew one style of martial arts.

Another one of the slogans of the early fight promoters was, "There are no rules." But, of course there were rules, such as no eye gouging. More and more rules came into play as mixed martial arts sought respectability and acceptance as a legitimate sport.

In the Ultimate Fighting Championship (UFC), fighters compete inside a cage called the *octagon*. It is an eight-sided structure, with a chain-linked fence that is six feet (1.8 m) high. Fighters compete in one of five weight classes, from lightweight to heavyweight. Each round is five minutes long. Title matches, where contestants fight for the championship of their weight class, are five rounds long. Non-title matches have three rounds. There is a one-minute rest period between rounds.

Below: Two fighters compete inside the octagon, the signature arena of the Ultimate Fighting Championship (UFC) mixed martial arts organization.

How to Win

There are five ways to win a fight: the judges' scorecards, tapping out, throwing in the towel, knockout, or by the referee stopping the contest.

The first way to win a fight is to refer to the judges' scorecards. This happens when both fighters are still fighting by the end of the match. Judges must then decide who won the match. The UFC competition uses the same kind of scoring used in boxing. Three judges evaluate each round. They decide which fighter won that round. Fighters win a round if they land more strikes, have more takedowns, or are more aggressive. The winner of each round receives 10 points. The loser receives nine points or less. If the judges rate the round as a tie, both fighters receive 10 points. So, if one fighter wins each of the three rounds, the judges' score might be 30 to 27.

Judges don't always agree on who wins a round. Sometimes, when a fight is over, there is a "split decision." This means that two judges thought one fighter won, and the other judge thought the opposite fighter won. In that case, the majority rules, so the two judges elect the winner.

The second way to win a fight is when an opponent "taps out." This means that one of the fighters surrenders to prevent further injury. For example, if one fighter has the other fighter in a chokehold, the choked fighter might tap the mat, which signals to the referee that he is giving up. Another common tap-out situation is when one fighter has his opponent in a leg lock, twisting the foot to cause more and more pain. The opponent might tap out to prevent injury to his leg.

Another less common way to win is when a fighter's coach or manager stops the match. They do this by throwing a towel into the ring, which causes the referee to stop the match. This is called "throwing in the towel." Sometimes a competitor is too hurt or tired to fight effectively, but is too stubborn to give up. If the fighter continues to fight, serious injury might result. To prevent this, the manager or coach surrenders for the fighter.

The fourth way to win a fight is by knockout, or "KO." This is when one fighter lands a solid hit on his opponent, knocking him out cold. The fighter might be temporarily unconscious, or too groggy to continue.

Above: Mixed martial arts features a combination of striking and grappling. The fight often continues even when one competitor is knocked down.

The fifth way to win is by the referee stopping the fight. The referee watches very closely, monitoring the safety of the fighters. If one fighter becomes too tired or has been hit too many times, he may no longer be able to defend himself. If a fighter's safety is endangered, the referee stops the match to prevent injury. In this case, the winning fighter is awarded a technical knockout, or "TKO."

In some cases, a fighter might get a cut, or take a punch to the nose, resulting in bleeding. A doctor is always available to evaluate the wound. The doctor can also stop a fight if he or she believes that it would be unsafe for a fighter to continue. This is considered the same as a referee stopping a fight, and the victor is awarded a TKO.

TRAINING

Many mixed martial arts events have sprung up across the United States. It has become a popular way to compete and show off one's martial arts skills. It takes long hours of practice to learn mixed martial arts. Today, UFC fighters train every day, like a full-time job. Most fighters are sponsored by an organization. This means that the organization pays them a salary to train, and then they agree to wear a t-shirt or hat with the sponsor's name on it so that it is visible on television.

Schools for mixed martial arts training have sprung up across the United States. These schools, often under the leadership of a famous fighter, train groups of competitors all day, every day.

A typical MMA training day includes weightlifting, aerobics, and fighting in many different martial arts styles. Weightlifting increases muscle size and strength. With strong muscles, it's possible to hold an opponent longer or tighter. Aerobics is also a critical part of training. Running, jumping rope, or bicycling helps increase stamina so competitors can fight longer without getting tired. Mixed martial arts is such an intense activity that if fighters are not in top shape, they can run out of energy quickly. When fighters are breathing too heavily, and are too tired to fight well, it is often called "gassing out."

Finally, MMA fighters practice a variety of martial arts styles. They may practice wrestling so they can understand how to control an opponent on the ground. They may practice Brazilian jiu-jitsu to learn holds that will make opponents tap out. They may learn karate to practice their

punching and kicking. They may learn Muay Thai to get a better understanding of how to use their elbows and knees as weapons. MMA fighters learn many different styles from many different teachers in an effort to be well rounded. They need to know what to do when they are standing or when they are on the ground.

Some schools have unusual training techniques, such as mountain climbing. This builds a variety of little-used muscles. Another unusual training technique is to run with a harness while pulling someone on a bicycle. This helps to build cardio capacity.

Of course, the most common training technique is simply to fight. MMA fighters compete with other students, and other people at their school. They may spend hours each day on the mat, learning the best techniques to help them become champions.

Above: A fighter wins a match by putting his opponent into an arm bar, which is a type of joint lock.

GLOSSARY

Belt

Most modern martial arts schools use a system of colored belts to rank their students based on their abilities and length of training. Each school decides the exact order of belts, but most are similar in ranking. A typical school might start beginner students at white belt. From there, the students progress to gold belt, then green, purple, blue, red, and brown. The highest belt is black. It usually takes from three to five years of intense training to achieve a black belt.

Control

The ability of a fighter to score points without hitting his or her opponent too hard, which can cause injuries. Excessive contact can result in penalty points or even disqualification.

Freestyle Form

A form in which competitors emphasize acrobatic movements, such as leaps, backflips, and sumersaults. Freestyle forms have become increasingly popular at martial arts tournaments because they are so exciting to watch.

Intramural

An event or series of activities that happen within a single organization. In intramural martial arts tournaments, schools hold competitions for their students only. In contrast, open tournaments welcome students from many different martial arts schools.

Kata

Japanese word for form. A set of prearranged motions, like a dance, performed with speed, precision, and power.

Katana

A long, single-edged sword used by Japanese samurai. Finely crafted, the katana has a slight curve, making it suitable for slashing attacks. A katana is also called a samurai sword.

Muay Thai

A style of kickboxing that is very popular in the country of Thailand.

Nunchaku

A martial arts weapon made from two hard pieces of wood joined together by a chain or rope.

Point Fighting

Tournament fighting, or sparring, in which points are awarded for each technique that scores against an opponent.

Tapping Out

During a mixed martial arts match, when one fighter is being choked or is in intense pain, such as from a joint lock, he taps the mat with his hand. The referee immediately stops the fight. A smart fighter knows when to tap out: he loses the fight, but prevents injury.

TKO

A term used in boxing and mixed martial arts competitions that means "technical knockout." When a fighter is too injured or tired to continue, the referee stops the match and awards a TKO to the winner.

Wakizashi

A smaller version of the katana, or samurai sword. Both were carried by samurai, the warriors of medieval Japan. The wakizashi was useful for close combat, and for the grim suicide ritual of seppuku.

INDEX